FRANKLIN PARK PUBLIC LIBRARY
FRANKLIN PARK, ILL.

Each borrower is held responsible for all library
material drawn on his card and for fines
accruing on the same. No material will be
issued until such fine has been paid.

All injuries to library material beyond
reasonable wear and all losses shall be made
good to the satisfaction of the librarian.

Replacement costs will be
billed after 42 days overdue.

Jack Kirby Creator & Artist

by Sue Hamilton

Visit us at
www.abdopublishing.com

Published by ABDO Publishing Company, 4940 Viking Drive, Suite 622, Edina, Minnesota 55435.
Copyright ©2007 by Abdo Consulting Group, Inc. International copyrights reserved in all countries.
No part of this book may be reproduced in any form without written permission from the publisher.
ABDO & Daughters™ is a trademark and logo of ABDO Publishing Company.

Printed in the United States.

Editor: John Hamilton
Graphic Design: Sue Hamilton
Cover Design: Neil Klinepier
Cover Illustration: Courtesy Jack Kirby estate
Interior Photos and Illustrations: pp 1–32: All Marvel comic book character and cover images
used with permission of Marvel Entertainment, Inc.; All photos of Jack Kirby and his family used
with permission of the Jack Kirby estate; p 4 Manhattan Lower East Side street scene, AP/Wide
World; p 7 Boys Brotherhood Republic, Getty Images; p 8 Bob Kane, Getty Images; p 16 American
troops land on beach at Normandy, Digital Stock; p 21 Charles F. Murphy holding comic book
panels, Corbis.

Library of Congress Cataloging-in-Publication Data

Hamilton, Sue L., 1959-
  Jack Kirby / Sue Hamilton.
      p. cm. -- (Comic book creators)
  Includes bibliographical references and index.
  ISBN-13: 978-1-59928-298-5
  ISBN-10: 1-59928-298-4
  1. Kirby, Jack--Juvenile literature. 2. Cartoonists--United States--Biography--Juvenile literature.
I. Title. II. Series: Hamilton, Sue L., 1959- Comic book creators.

PN6727.K57Z63 2006
741.5092--dc22
[B]
                          2006015405

Contents

Jack "King" Kirby

Captain America. The Fantastic Four. The Incredible Hulk. The X-Men. The Mighty Thor. The Silver Surfer. These are just a few of the most popular comic book characters created by an amazing man named Jacob Kurtzberg. He was born on August 28, 1917. Although he would never be more than 5´ 4˝ tall, he would grow up to become the comic book world's legendary Jack "King" Kirby.

Born on the Lower East Side of New York's Manhattan Island, Jacob was the oldest child of Rose and Benjamin Kurtzberg. They were Jewish immigrants who had left their native Austria, arriving in America seeking freedom and opportunity. Benjamin Kurtzberg worked as a tailor in a factory, making men's suits. Rose found work wherever she could. She was also an avid storyteller, and from the time her son was born, she told him stories and legends from the old country. With this introduction, the boy learned how to create an exciting story. But Jacob's real life was more about surviving from day-to-day.

Jacob's nickname was "Jakie." Every neighborhood had its own group, and Jakie became a member of the Suffolk Street Gang. Their "fun" included getting into fights—everywhere from the streets to the rooftops to the fire escapes. Jakie also got into fights protecting his brother, David, who was five years younger.

As Jacob grew up during the Great Depression, he had to work to help support his family. He sold newspapers, although he admitted he was never very good at it. He also got small jobs running errands for people. He had to do whatever he could to earn money.

Below: Early 20th century pushcart vendors sell their merchandise along the sidewalk of Manhattan's Lower East Side.

Above: A young Jack Kirby with his parents, Rose and Benjamin Kurtzberg.

The Teenage Artist

Jacob Kurtzberg's experiences on the street made him tough, but he used his hands for something more than just making fists. He drew pictures. His creative and artistic talents showed up early. He would later state, "I was there in the shadow of the chipped brick walls of the slum, my first drawing board." He began to check out "how-to-draw" books from the library. He doodled on scraps of paper. He went to Saturday afternoon movies and watched his heroes. He read science fiction books. All of this helped him learn how to create an exciting story.

One day after school he found a pulp magazine in the street called *Wonder Stories*. The huge, colorful pictures of rocket ships and adventurous characters changed everything for him. He wanted to create art like that!

In 1931, at the age of 14, Jacob went to art school at the Pratt Institute in New York. He lasted there a week. His father had lost his job, and the family couldn't afford to pay for the young artist to attend the school. But Jacob wasn't exactly the type of "fine artist" the school was teaching. He had his own style, and rather than have formal training, he continued to teach himself.

As a teen, he became a cartoonist for the *Boys Brotherhood Republic,* a newspaper for young people created by Harry Slonaker, a social worker who wanted to help boys learn useful skills and responsibility. At age 16, Kurtzberg became the newspaper's artist, and produced his own comic strip, called *K's Konceptions.*

Below: The cover of the October 1931 issue of *Wonder Stories,* edited by Hugo Gernsback, with artwork by Frank R. Paul.

Above: Jack Kirby's drawing test of Popeye for Max Fleischer's animation studio. Working as an "in-betweener," Kirby completed the motion in between the three "key" frames drawn by the chief animator.

The fighting on the street continued, and Jacob wanted an out. He didn't want to be poor anymore. He wanted something more, and it looked like his talent could do it for him. As Jacob got older, work and money became much more important to the Kurtzberg family. In 1935, the young Kurtzberg quit high school in the beginning of his senior year to take a job as an "in-betweener" with Max Fleischer's animation studio. An in-betweener drew the pictures between "key" drawings. Jack's test to get the job required him to draw the picture of cartoon character Popeye's leg taking a step. He could do it easily.

Jacob kept the job for two years, but it was the same thing day after day. He hated the work, but it gave him practice. It also gave him something that would help him greatly in the future: speed at drawing. With this experience, he began looking for something new to do with his talents, and he soon found it.

Left: A Boys Brotherhood Republic in New York City, where troubled boys, including gang members, could find shelter from the harsh conditions of the streets, or even learn useful job skills. As a teenager, Jack Kirby became a cartoonist for the *Boys Brotherhood Republic* newspaper.

Opposites Attract

Lincoln Features Syndicate created newspaper cartoons and comic strips. At the age of 19, Jacob began working for them. Here, he drew everything from pirates (*Black Buccaneer*) and sailors (*Socco the Sea Dog*), to detectives (*Abdul Jones*) and Western cowboys (*The Lone Rider*). The boy from the Lower East Side was quickly becoming an all-around talented artist.

It was during this time that a momentous event occurred: In June 1938, the new *Action Comics* #1 was published, featuring Superman. It took a few months, but by issue #7, it was a sell-out! Almost overnight, comic books became big business, and Jacob wanted in on the action.

He carried his portfolio of work over to Art Syndication Company, and got a job as a comic book artist, working for Will Eisner and Jerry Iger. Here, Jacob would produce his first comic book, which was called *Wild Boy Magazine*. He also worked on an oversized comic book called *Jumbo*. In addition, he turned out science fiction (*Diary of Dr. Hayward*) and adventure (*The Count of Monte Cristo*).

Jacob worked with several future comic book legends, including Bob Kahn, who would later change his name to Bob Kane and create Batman. But it was his next move, to Fox Publications, that really helped move Jacob Kurtzberg into fame.

Below: Bob Kane, creator of Batman. Jack Kirby worked with Kane as a comic book artist for Art Syndication Company in the late 1930s.

Above: Jack Kirby as a young man, hard at work on his drawing table.

Above: Jack Kirby drew this panel for the comic strip, *The Blue Beetle*, which ran on January 27, 1940. Charles Nicholas was a "house" name used by several artists who worked for Fox Publications.

Now 21 years old, Jacob had been working for several months for Victor Fox, when a tall, skinny young man by the name of Joe Simon was hired as the senior editor for the company. The two were quite opposite. Where Jacob was short and somewhat wide (from his love of sweets), Joe was nearly a foot taller and very thin. Jacob earned the small sum of $15 a week; Joe earned $85 a week as editor-in-chief. Jacob spent most of his time on the art, and while Joe was an artist, he was also a businessman and a dealmaker. But the two worked together well, and when Jacob, who was still helping to support his family, asked Joe for freelance work that Jacob could do at night, an amazing partnership was born.

Together, Jacob and Joe rented a one-room office. They began working nights and weekends on such comics as *The Blue Beetle*, a crime-fighter whose bulletproof beetle costume was quite unique. Jacob's history on the streets and his time as an in-betweener served him well, as he quickly created art that showed real action, not just someone throwing a punch.

Working on the side, Jacob was paid 10 times what he made at Fox Publications. But he continued working his day job at $15 a week. It was steady work that helped his family. But Jacob Kurtzberg would finally make a major change.

Right: In this 1945 photo, Jack Kirby is seen standing on the left, with his friend and creative partner, Joe Simon, on the right. In the middle is Alfred Harvey, who later went on to start Harvey Comics, publisher of such favorites as *Casper the Friendly Ghost* and *Richie Rich*.

During the early 1940s, Jack Kirby and Joe Simon worked together on many popular comic book creations. Clockwise, from left: *Champion Comics* #8, June 1940; *Red Raven* #1, August 1940; *Blue Bolt* #3, August 1940 (the first Kirby & Simon collaboration); *Speed Comics* #19, June 1942.

Captain America is Born

During his time as an artist, Jacob invented a number of pseudonyms—fictitious names—for himself: Fred Sande, Michael Griffith, Jack Curtiss, Floyd Kelly, Lance Kirby, Curt Davis, Jack Cortez. He didn't want Victor Fox to know that he was freelancing, and he wanted his name to sound more "American." So he used false names.

Finally, in the fall of 1939, he quit Fox's company. A few days later, he went down to City Hall and officially changed his name to Jack Kirby. His parents didn't like it, but this was close to his real name, and it would be the name that millions of comic book fans would come to know.

Joe Simon was now working with Martin Goodman at Timely Comics. Simon brought Jack in as a co-creator and artist. (Timely would eventually become Marvel Comics some 20 years later.) Joe and Jack created a success for Timely in March 1940 with The Vision, a mystical green-suited hero who appeared wherever there was smoke. The idea was born when the two men smoked cigars in their small office.

Below: Jack and Roz Kirby at a cafe in Brooklyn, New York, in 1945.

By this time, Jack's family had moved to a home in Brooklyn, New York. They lived on the first floor. New neighbors soon arrived to live on the second floor. Rosalind "Roz" Goldstein was nearly 18 when her family moved in. Jack, who was 23 at the time, introduced himself, offering to show her his etchings. She didn't know what "etchings" were, but quickly discovered the young man's drawings were wonderful. They began dating.

Above: Jack Kirby at the New York World's Fair in 1939.

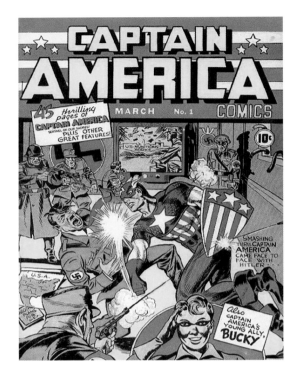

Above: Captain America #1, showing Captain America slugging Adolf Hitler.

Facing page: A Jack Kirby illustration of Captain America.

Jack may have been lucky with love, but he and Joe were having a creative dry spell. Nothing had really taken off for the pair since *The Vision.* It was during this time that Nazi Germany's Adolf Hitler marched soldiers all across Europe. Everyone hated this real-life villain, and that gave Joe Simon an idea. Joe wanted a hero who could take on and defeat Hitler. So was born Captain America. Martin Goodman wasn't sure this was a great idea. Half of the world was out to get this guy, and Hitler could be dead by the time the comic book was out on newsstands.

But Joe and Jack moved ahead. With a red, white, and blue costume covering bulging muscles, this heroic figure entered the world of comics in December 1940 (although the issue was dated March 1941). The cover featured Captain America giving Hitler a knockout punch to the jaw. A million copies were sold. Nearly overnight, *Captain America* was a super success. As Joe Simon said, "We were entertaining the world."

With this success, the two closed down their small office and Jack went to work at Timely as the company's art director. Their freelancing didn't end, however. They worked on Fawcett Publications' *Captain Marvel.* Once again, they helped produce a comic book that was a huge success.

Throughout 1941, the twosome created successes such as *USA, All-Winners,* and *Young Allies,* each selling nearly a million copies a month. However, on December 7, 1941, Japanese planes attacked the United States Naval Base at Pearl Harbor, Hawaii. Jack and Roz heard about it when leaving the theater that evening. As they walked out, the usually busy, happy street was filled with worried, concerned people. They quickly learned what had happened. The next day, America declared war on Japan, and Jack Kirby's life would soon change dramatically.

15

Love and War

On May 23, 1942, Jack Kirby married Roz. Jack and Joe Simon continued to successfully create comics such as *The Boy Commandos*, stories about kid gangs who took on Nazis and other evildoers who posed a threat to America. Financially, Jack Kirby was doing well. He and Roz moved into their own apartment in Manhattan Beach, New York.

On June 7, 1943, Jack received a telegram from the United States government—he had been drafted into the Army. Since Jack was married, as well as helping care for his parents by giving them money, he hadn't been recruited in the beginning of the war. But he had known it would be coming. Joe Simon had joined the Coast Guard a few months earlier.

Jack was part of the combat infantry. After a trip across the Atlantic Ocean, his outfit reached Normandy, France, on June 16, 1944. Ten days earlier, on D-Day, nearly 3 million Allied troops had fought one of the largest battles of World War II. Landing on the coast of France, his outfit marched across Omaha Beach, which was still covered with the bodies of thousands of soldiers. Jack would never forget the horror.

Right: On D-Day, June 6, 1944, American troops landed on the beach of Normandy, France. It was one of the largest battles of World War II.

All his years of brawling on the streets served him well. Jack was a good fighter. His outfit was under the command of the famous General George S. Patton. They moved constantly so the German soldiers would get no rest. Of course, the Americans never rested either. But at least by always moving, they stayed warm.

One day, Jack was called upon to use his artistic skills. A lieutenant in the command center found out that Jack was the comic book artist who drew *Captain America* and *The Boy Commandos*. At first Jack thought the man wanted a portrait. Instead, he found out that he was needed as an advance scout. Kirby was ordered to go into specific towns and draw maps and pictures of the area and any high-ranking soldiers or officials he saw there. It was a dangerous job. Basically, Jack was asked to be a spy.

Above: Jack Kirby in uniform, during World War II.

Jack's days were filled with fighting, spying, drawing, and surviving. He never liked Army life. He wrote letters to Roz, which included small pictures of the people around him. Sometimes, those people were dead by the time Roz received the letters.

Private Jack Kirby was always near the action. One winter, his feet froze, and his legs turned into what he described as purple "elephant legs." He was sent to a hospital in London, England. His buddies, whose legs were black, lost their limbs. Jack's legs were purple, and he eventually recovered.

At the start of 1945, Jack was sent home by boat. He felt lucky. Others aboard the ship had lost hands, legs, fingers, noses, and ears. In May 1945, Germany surrendered. Jack was honorably discharged on July 20, 1945. In August 1945, atomic bombs were dropped on Japan. On September 2, Japan officially surrendered. World War II was over and Jack Kirby had survived.

Kids and Comics

Jack and Roz Kirby became proud parents of a baby daughter, named Susan, on December 6, 1945. Jack was back in the comics business, teaming with Joe Simon, who had also survived the war years.

Once again, this was a boom time for comics. Kirby and Simon did well together. Their characters were very popular. They cut deals with their publisher that gave them 50 percent of the profits. Together, they produced *Justice Traps the Guilty*, a crime comic. They also created *Boy Explorers*, with stories similar to *The Boy Commandos*.

Money was good in the business, but there was a whole group of readers out there that nobody was reaching: females. Publishers wanted comic books that girls could read. Jack and Joe created *Young Romance*. In 1947, the first issue sold a million copies. Following issues, with titles such as "Misguided Heart" and "Boy Crazy," became top sellers.

The two men, along with their families, moved into houses across the street from each other on Long Island, New York. Each had a studio in their house, and they worked out of each other's homes, coming up with ideas for their next great adventure.

Below: Jack and Roz Kirby, with their son, Neal, and daughter Susan, in front of their home on Long Island, NY, in the late 1940s.

Above: Jack Kirby in uniform in 1945, home from the battlefields of Europe.

Right: Jack Kirby proofing comic book covers in his office in 1949.

Below: Examples of comic books produced by the team of Jack Kirby and Joe Simon in the late 1940s and early 1950s.

Both their business and personal lives were busy. Jack's son, Neal, was born on May 25, 1948. *Young Love* was added to their romance line in 1949. Westerns were again popular, so in October 1950, Jack's soon-to-be-successful Western comic, *Boys' Ranch*, was published. A daughter, Barbara, came along on November 29, 1952. Jack was home to help Roz with the kids during the day, and then worked at night when everyone was asleep. Jack never slowed down, penciling as much as three pages of comics a night. Joe and Jack wanted more business, so in early 1954 they started their own publishing company, Mainline Comics. Their creations included *Bullseye: Western Scout*, *In Love*, *Police Trap*, and *Foxhole*.

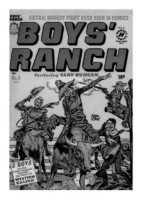

Business was steady for Jack. But in 1954, a doctor named Fredric Wertham released a book, *Seduction of the Innocent*, which blamed comics for ruining kids' lives. The United States Senate began investigating comics. The comic book business was badly hurt.

To stop the loss of business, most comic book publishers agreed in 1954 to be part of a new group called the Comics Magazine Association of America. The association was in charge of the Comics Code Authority, which created guidelines to make sure comics weren't too violent.

If a comic was approved, it was awarded a seal of approval, which was printed on the front cover. It was a form of self-censorship, but comic book companies followed the rules to stay in business. Without the seal of approval, most stores and newsstands refused to sell the comics.

Even though comics became less violent, sales continued to decrease because of the controversy. Mainline Comics, Joe and Jack's new publishing company, soon went out of business. After that, Joe Simon went to work in the advertising industry. But Jack Kirby continued to create comics. His most exciting years were still ahead of him.

Above: Judge Charles F. Murphy, administrator of the Comics Magazine Association of America, holds a group of comic books "approved" by the Comics Code Authority.

APPROVED
BY THE
COMICS
CODE
AUTHORITY

The Silver Age of Comics

For the rest of the 1950s, Jack Kirby continued creating comics. On September 6, 1960, his youngest daughter, Lisa, was born. With a family of four kids to support, Jack had to stay busy. He worked on *Western Tales*, featuring Davy Crockett and Jim Bowie, as well as the mystery series *Black Cat Mystic*. He produced romances such as *Young Brides*, *First Love*, and *First Romance*. When bug-eyed monsters (BEM's) and aliens became popular, Jack created *Tales of the Unexpected*, and *Challengers of the Unknown*.

Jack worked with such popular comic book companies as Harvey, Atlas, and National, which later became DC Comics. But it would be Martin Goodman's Atlas, soon to be called Marvel Comics, that some of Kirby's greatest work would come to light.

Jack had been working at Atlas when publisher Martin Goodman brought on board his wife's cousin, Stanley Lieber, in 1941. Stanley changed his name to Stan Lee, and soon became the head editor of the company. He and Jack worked on many projects together.

After Martin Goodman learned that National Comics' *The Justice League* was doing so well, he asked for a comic book with a "super team." Stan and Jack came up with the characters. Then Jack brought them to life with his artistic skills. The result was *The Fantastic Four,* which included Mr. Fantastic, Invisible Woman, Human Torch, and The Thing. Using his love of science fiction for inspiration, Jack had fun creating the weird and unique characters. But it was The Thing that he would later say was most like himself—a tough fighter with a kind heart.

Below: Fantastic Four #1, November 1961, with pencil artwork by Jack Kirby and story by Stan Lee.

Above: Jack Kirby poses in front of a framed piece of artwork featuring his drawings for *The Fantastic Four.*

Above: Jack Kirby hard at work in his studio in 1965.

The comic book hit shelves in late autumn, 1961. It was a fantastic success. With success came money for Marvel Comics, and with money came more work for Jack.

Jack continued working on *The Fantastic Four*, as well as Westerns, romances, and aliens. Then he and Stan Lee created a type of Dr. Jeckyl/Mr. Hyde character. Jack heard a story of a woman whose child was caught under a car. In her panic, she gained superhuman strength to lift the car and free the child. Jack and Stan combined that tale with the fictional character of Frankenstein's monster. Their story involved a scientist named Bruce Banner, who was exposed to gamma rays in an experiment gone bad. Afterwards, whenever Banner got mad, he turned into an incredibly strong, green-skinned monster who took on crooks and villains. *The Incredible Hulk* hit stands in May 1962. Once again, Kirby and Stan Lee had produced a hit.

Everything was going very well at Marvel, and the success was to continue. Editor Stan Lee came up with an idea for a spider-like character. Artist Steve Ditko was called in to work on the illustrations for the first story. Jack produced the first Spider-Man cover, which was introduced in the *Amazing Fantasy* comic book of August 1962. It was another smash hit for Marvel.

Although Jack didn't work on the Spider-Man stories at this time, he continued to do some of the covers. Jack was becoming famous in the world of comic book art, and he was a very busy man. In the comic book *Journey into Mystery,* Jack drew The Mighty Thor, the Norse god of thunder. As a boy, Jack's mom told him the legends of their Scandinavian homeland. Jack enjoyed creating the god's imaginative home of Asgard. Clever, futuristic buildings floated on a cloud set in deep space. Stan and Jack built stories around this world of immortals. Three years later, in March 1966, the team's hard work paid off when Thor was given his own comic book.

Above: Jack Kirby posing with a costumed Spider-Man at a comics convention.

Above: Sgt. Fury and his Howling Commandos, #5, January 1964.

Below: Jack Kirby at work, surrounded by several of his comic book creations.

In May 1963, Jack's military experience came in handy when he started working on a new comic, *Sgt. Fury and his Howling Commandos*. Jack grew very good at drawing groups of comic book characters. Because of this valuable experience, Kirby was given the job of drawing Marvel's next big creation: *The X-Men*.

Introduced in September 1963, this group of super-powered mutant teens with "X-tra" powers was led by wheelchair-bound Professor Charles Xavier. Jack used his drawing talents to design some of the most unique characters ever produced in a comic book. Cyclops was a smart young man, whose eyes emitted force beams. Iceman was a teen with the power to freeze moisture in the air. Archangel had wings growing from his shoulder blades that allowed him to fly. Beast was a strong, ape-like genius. And Marvel Girl (Jean Grey) was a young woman with the power of telekinesis.

Next came the evil mutants, lead by Magneto, a genius who could control magnetic waves. Then came Toad, Mastermind, Scarlet Witch, and Quicksilver. Each character received Jack's special artistic talents, and these were just a few of the many X-Men developed over the years.

Jack worked on another major comic in 1963, called *The Avengers*. Taking some of Marvel's most popular "long-underwear characters," Jack drew them together as a new team. The first adventure featured Thor, Iron Man, Antman, Wasp, and The Incredible Hulk. The group teamed up to battle Loki, an evildoer from Thor's homeland of Asgard.

The 1960s are often referred to as the Silver Age of Comics. Amazingly, Jack Kirby produced 1,492 comic books, covers, and character posters in that decade alone. He never missed a month of production, and time after time created amazing stories and characters.

Above: Jack Kirby at a comic book convention in the 1980s.

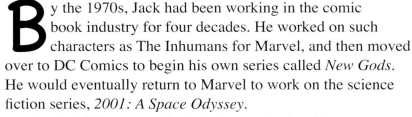

The King of Comics

By the 1970s, Jack had been working in the comic book industry for four decades. He worked on such characters as The Inhumans for Marvel, and then moved over to DC Comics to begin his own series called *New Gods*. He would eventually return to Marvel to work on the science fiction series, *2001: A Space Odyssey*.

As the 1980s approached, Jack went back to his beginnings, working in animation, creating storyboards for cartoons, but still producing comic books. Now in his 60s, Jack was getting tired. He was still doing more work every day than most younger artists, but he had health problems. Jack had been a smoker all his life, and this eventually resulted in throat cancer. Also, his eyesight was failing, and he had to undergo heart bypass surgery.

However, it wasn't just physical problems that made him heartsick. After decades of drawing thousands of pages of comics, which were now worth quite a lot of money, he wanted his artwork back. He created the art, and felt that he alone owned it. But he wasn't fighting just for himself. He wanted companies to understand that art could be used, but it was still owned by the creator. Jack fought to get his artwork back from Marvel and DC. Eventually, a small portion was returned, but the fight had taken a lot of energy out of him.

As Jack entered his 70s, his health continued to fail, but his popularity continued. He was always one to encourage young artists. During comic book conventions, he continued to thank the many people who showered him with praise and admiration. Jack was a legend. On February 6, 1994, the legend passed into history.

Since Kirby's death, several of his characters, including The X-Men, The Incredible Hulk, and The Fantastic Four, have been featured in movies. Comic book lovers still consider him the master. Kirby once said, "My stories began to get noticed because the average reader could associate with them."

Above: Jack Kirby, the king of comics, in 1991.

His co-creator Stan Lee said, "Nobody drew a strip like Jack Kirby. He was not only a great artist, he was also a great visual storyteller." Lee nicknamed him Jack "King" Kirby. Millions of fans agreed that Kirby was the king of comics. But most of all, he was a hard-working man of vision.

Glossary

CENSORSHIP
The control of what is written or spoken by a central authority, often a government or large group of outspoken individuals.

CO-CREATOR
A person working with another person to make up a comic book character. Especially in the comic book area, often a writer and an artist work together to develop a character's story, as well as its look, outfit, and special abilities.

COMICS CODE AUTHORITY (CCA)
Established in 1954 as a way for comic book publishers to deal with parents' concerns about the effects of crime and horror comics on kids. Every comic book published required the CCA's seal of approval, and had to follow a strict set of guidelines. The Code is still in use today, although not all comic books are published with the CCA seal.

CREATOR
A person who thinks up the personality, physical look, and special skills of a comic book character.

GREAT DEPRESSION
A time in America's history beginning in 1929 and lasting for several years, when the stock market crashed, resulting in business failures across the country and the loss of jobs for millions of Americans.

ILLUSTRATE
To add a piece of art to a printed story. The art may be a drawing, painting, or photo.

IMMIGRANTS

People who move from one country to another, taking the new country as their home.

PSEUDONYM

A fake name often used by writers and artists who do not want to use their real name for various reasons. Also called a "pen name."

PULP MAGAZINES

A nickname for fiction magazines published on the cheapest possible paper made from wood pulp. Also called "the pulps."

SUPERHEROES

Characters, often human, but they may also be alien or mythological beings, who develop or have special skills that give them superhuman powers. These characters use their powers for good, helping and protecting people.

WORLD WAR II

A war that was fought from 1939 to 1945, involving countries around the world. The United States entered the war after Japan's bombing of the American naval base at Pearl Harbor, in Oahu, Hawaii, on December 7, 1941.

Above: Jack and Roz Kirby at their home in November, 1989.

Index